THE TAO OF SWAYZE

PHILLIP CALLAWAY
FOREWORD BY ESCHER SMALLWATER

Nobody Puts Swayze in the Corner: the Tao of Swayze Copyright©2007 by Marcus Eder. All rights reserved. Printed in the United States of America. No part of this book may be used or reproduced in any manner whatsoever without express written consent from the author. He'll probably give it to ya, if you ask nicely.

 Vicious Books First Paperback Edition, 2008
(www.viciousbooks.com)

10 9 8 7 6 5 4 3 2 1 (boom)

Cover design and book layout by Marcus Eder
About the font used: Futura is a geometric sans-serif typeface designed in 1927 by Paul Renner. Although Renner was not associated with the Bauhaus, he shared many of its idioms and believed that a modern typeface should express modern models, rather than be a revival of a previous design. Renner's initial design included several geometrically constructed alternative characters and ranging (old style) figures which can be found in the typeface Architype Renner. Futura was commissioned by the Bauer type foundry. -Wikipedia

ISBN 978-0-9820198-1-8

No animals were harmed in the making of this book.

THIS BOOK IS DEDICATED TO ANYONE
WHO HAS BEEN TOUCHED BY CANCER.

TOGETHER WE CAN FIND A CURE.

FOREWORD
BY ESCHER SMALLWATER

I'm a sucker for the internet. It allows me to write as if I were educated beyond my years–to speak on any variety of subjects I know nothing about with a certain level of confidence and authority. With a simple point and click of the mouse I have all the information I need to craft a foreword that, on the surface, would seem quite educated and credible.

In truth, I'm a hack.

I'm neither a philosopher nor a writer; merely an unemployed graphic designer who found a completed transcript sitting next to a bottle of Jack Daniels in the oven of a dead friend. There was also a note:

"Either we drink in celebration or you drink in my honor"

Sadly, it was the latter. How he died is a fantastic story, and one I highly recommend.

But the pages of this particular book do not tell that story.

Phillip Callaway lived below me in South City, St. Louis. He used to be a copywriter for the same agency I worked at.

He was laid off the week after me.

The night of his dismissal, we watched, only half surprised, as Phil carried his PC into the backyard, doused it in lighter fluid, screamed some profanities and lit up the night.

For months he sat in front of an old typewriter rescued from the dumpster behind our flat, typing away at odd hours of the morning, day and night. Fueled by bourbon, coffee and nicotine, Phil attempted to write a definitive, life-affirming book for a generation of slackers and the post nukes nipping at their heels.

He also watched a lot of Cable TV.

And this is where Nobody Puts Swayze in the Corner: the Tao of Swayze was born.

The Tao itself translates as "way," "path," or "route," or sometimes more loosely as "doctrine" or "principle." It is used philosophically to signify the fundamental or true nature of the world. The concept of Tao is an active and holistic conception of the world, rather than the static, atomistic view found in western philosophy.

Wikipedia defines The Tao Te Ching as a "Chinese classic text, its name stemming from the opening words of its two sections: dào "way," Chapter 1, and dé "virtue." According to tradition, it was written around the 6th century BCE by the Taoist sage Laozi (or Lao Tzu, "Old Master"), a record-keeper at the Zhou Dynasty court, by whose name the text is known in China. The text's true authorship and date of composition or compilation are still debated.

The Tao Te Ching is fundamental to the Taoist school of Chinese philosophy and strongly influenced other schools, such as Legalism and Neo-Confucianism. This ancient book is also central in Chinese religion, not only for Taoism, but Chinese Buddhism, which when first introduced into China was largely interpreted through the use of Taoist words and concepts. Many Chinese artists, including poets, painters, calligraphers, and even gardeners have used the Tao Te Ching as a source of inspiration. Its influence has also spread widely outside East Asia, aided by hundreds of translations into Western languages.

In Taoism, Tao both precedes and encompasses the universe. As with other nondualistic philosophies, all the observable objects in the Tao Te Ching are considered to be manifestations of Tao, and can only operate within the Tao's principles. Tao by contrast is often referred to as 'the nameless,' because neither it nor its principles can ever be adequately expressed in words. It has no shape or form, is simultaneously perfectly still and constantly moving, is both larger than the largest thing and smaller than the smallest, and in general is outside of all dichotomies.

While the Tao cannot be expressed, Taoism holds that it can be known, and its principles can be followed. Much of Taoist writing focuses on the value of following the Tao - called Te, or virtue - and of the ultimate uselessness of trying to control Tao outright. This is often expressed through yin and yang arguments, where every action creates a counter-action as a natural, unavoidable movement within manifestations of the Tao. Tao is often compared to water: clear, colorless, unremarkable, yet all beings depend on it for life, and even the hardest stone cannot stand in its way forever." (wikipedia)

Phil felt the same inherent truths, the same path are also in the prolific words found in the classic movies of actor, Patrick Swayze. From his first appearance on the big screen in the role of Ace, a cocky, roller-disco king in the hit movie, *Skate Town USA*, Swayze has enchanted and enlightened the world with sage-like wisdom.

This wisdom has carried through every movie he's made since, from obscure, independent films such as *Donnie Darko* and *To Wong Foo, Thanks for Everything Julie Newmar*, to undeniable blockbusters like *Point Break*, and *Dirty Dancing*.

This book attempts to pair the passages of the Tao with quotes from Swayze's movies; to blend the inherent truths found on the path to an enlightened life. The Taoist quotes on the left page are a reflection of Swayze's words on the right.

You can judge for yourself, it's all nothing more than a Rorschach test on the ribcage of life.

In light of Patrick Swayze's battle with Pancreatic Cancer, it seems only fitting that the proceeds from this book should benefit the American Cancer Society. It would be rude not to, really.

Kindest Regards,

Escher

NOBODY PUTS SWAYZE IN THE CORNER
THE TAO OF SWAYZE

**WHO DISTINGUISHES HIMSELF FROM THE WORLD
MAY BE GIVEN THE WORLD,
BUT WHO REGARDS HIMSELF AS THE WORLD
MAY ACCEPT THE WORLD.**

十三

We can exist on a different **plane,** we can make **our own rules.**

—the Book of Bodhi

A GENERAL IS WELL ADVISED TO ACHIEVE NOTHING MORE THAN HIS ORDERS: NOT TO TAKE ADVANTAGE OF HIS VICTORY. NOR TO GLORY, BOAST OR PRIDE HIMSELF; TO DO WHAT IS DICTATED BY NECESSITY, BUT NOT BY CHOICE.

All you have to do is follow three simple rules. One, never underestimate your opponent. Expect the unexpected. Two, take it outside. Never start anything inside the bar unless it's absolutely necessary. And three, be nice.

---the Book of Dalton

HEALTH OR REPUTATION: WHICH IS HELD DEARER?
HEALTH OR POSSESSIONS: WHICH HAS MORE WORTH?
PROFIT OR LOSS: WHICH IS MORE TROUBLESOME?

GREAT LOVE INCURS GREAT EXPENSE,
AND GREAT RICHES INCUR GREAT FEAR,

BUT CONTENTMENT COMES AT NO COST;

四十四

If you want the ultimate, you've got to be willing to pay the ultimate price.

---the Book of Bodhi

SO SOME WILL LEAD, WHILE OTHERS FOLLOW.
SOME WILL BE WARM, OTHERS COLD
SOME WILL BE STRONG, OTHERS WEAK.
SOME WILL GET WHERE THEY ARE GOING
WHILE OTHERS FALL BY THE SIDE OF THE ROAD.

二十九

Is that all the gusta you can musta?

—the Book of Darko

**GOOD FORTUNE FOLLOWS UPON DISASTER;
DISASTER LURKS WITHIN GOOD FORTUNE;
WHO CAN SAY HOW THINGS WILL END?
PERHAPS THERE IS NO END.**

五十八

It'll get worse before it gets better.

—the Book of Dalton

THE WAY IS THE FATE OF MEN,
THE TREASURE OF THE SAINT,
AND THE REFUGE OF THE SINNER.

FINE WORDS ARE OFTEN BORROWED,
GREAT DEEDS ARE OFTEN APPROPRIATED.

It takes a real saint to ask daddy.

—the Book of Johnny Castle

THE RIVER CARVES OUT THE VALLEY BY FLOWING BENEATH IT. THEREBY THE RIVER IS THE MASTER OF THE VALLEY.

六十六

Why be a servant to the law when you can be its master?

—the Book of Bodhi

WHEN BEAUTY IS ABSTRACTED, THEN UGLINESS HAS BEEN IMPLIED; WHEN GOOD IS ABSTRACTED THEN EVIL HAS BEEN IMPLIED.

THE SAGE EXPERIENCES WITHOUT ABSTRACTION, AND ACCOMPLISHES WITHOUT ACTION; HE ACCEPTS THE EBB AND FLOW OF THINGS, NURTURES THEM, BUT DOES NOT OWN THEM, AND LIVES, BUT DOES NOT DWELL.

二

We shouldn't just look into the mirror, we should look through the mirror.

―the Book of Darko

**NOT PRAISING THE WORTHY PREVENTS CONTENTION,
NOT ESTEEMING THE VALUABLE PREVENTS THEFT,
NOT DISPLAYING THE BEAUTIFUL PREVENTS DESIRE.**

**IF PEOPLE LACK KNOWLEDGE AND DESIRE THEN THEY
CAN NOT ACT; IF NO ACTION IS TAKEN HARMONY REMAINS.**

The way to screw up somebody's life is to give them what they want.

—the Book of Patrick

**NATURE IS NOT KIND; IT TREATS ALL THINGS IMPARTIALLY.
THE SAGE IS NOT KIND, AND TREATS ALL PEOPLE IMPARTIALLY.**

五

Everything moves in cycles; so twice a century the ocean let's us know just how small we really are.

---the Book of Bodhi

NATURE IS COMPLETE BECAUSE IT DOES NOT SERVE ITSELF.

**THE SAGE STAYS BEHIND AND FINDS HIMSELF AHEAD,
HE IS DETACHED AND THEREFORE ONE WITH ALL**

It's kind of strange, isn't it? How the mountains pay us no attention at all. You laugh or you cry...The wind just keeps on blowing.

---the Book of Jed

THESE BEHAVIOURS ARE WASTEFUL, INDULGENT, AND SO THEY ATTRACT DISFAVOUR;

HARMONY AVOIDS THEM.

二十四

You smoke more than a pack today and I'll skin you, you understand?

---the Book of Darry

WITH BUT A SMALL UNDERSTANDING
ONE MAY FOLLOW THE WAY LIKE A MAIN ROAD,
FEARING ONLY TO LEAVE IT;
FOLLOWING A MAIN ROAD IS EASY,
YET PEOPLE DELIGHT IN DIFFICULT PATHS

五十三

Maps are for cheaters

—the Book of Vida

**IF PEOPLE WERE NOT AFRAID OF DEATH,
THEN WHAT WOULD BE THE USE OF AN EXECUTIONER?**

七十四

Fear causes hesitation, and hesitation will cause your worst fears to come true.

—the Book of Bodhi

**GOOD WEAPONS ARE INSTRUMENTS OF FEAR;
ALL CREATURES HATE THEM.**

三十一

Once you get them **peeing** down their leg, they submit.

---the Book of Dalton

BY OPENING YOUR HEART, YOU BECOME ACCEPTED; ACCEPTING THE WORLD, YOU EMBRACE THE WAY.

十

Learn to truly love yourself and the world will be yours.

—the Book of Darko

POWERFUL MEN ARE WELL ADVISED NOT TO USE VIOLENCE,
FOR VIOLENCE HAS A HABIT OF RETURNING;
THORNS AND WEEDS GROW WHEREVER AN ARMY GOES,
AND LEAN YEARS FOLLOW A GREAT WAR.

三十

If somebody gets in your face and calls you a cocksucker, I want you to be nice.

---the Book of Dalton

BENEATH SENSATION AND MEMORY, THE WAY IS THE SOURCE OF ALL THE WORLD.

HOW CAN ONE UNDERSTAND THE SOURCE OF THE WORLD?

BY ACCEPTING.

Shit
happens

—the Book of Bodhi

**PEOPLE OFTEN FAIL ON THE VERGE OF SUCCESS;
TAKE CARE AT THE END AS AT THE BEGINNING,
SO THAT YOU MAY AVOID FAILURE.**

六十四

I'm balancing on shit and I can be down there again.

—the Book of Johnny Castle

THERE IS NO GREATER MISTAKE THAN FOLLOWING DESIRE;
THERE IS NO GREATER DISASTER THAN FORGETTING CONTENTMENT;
THERE IS NO GREATER SICKNESS THAN SEEKING ATTAINMENT;
BUT ONE WHO IS CONTENT TO SATISFY HIS NEEDS
FINDS THAT CONTENTMENT ENDURES.

You're too stupid to have a good time

—the Book of Dalton

THE PEOPLE ARE BUSY WITH PURPOSE,
WHERE I AM IMPRACTICAL AND ROUGH;
I DO NOT SHARE THE PEOPLES' CARES
BUT I AM FED AT NATURE'S BREAST.

Just put your **pickle** on everybody's plate and leave the hard stuff to me.

—the Book of Johnny Castle

NATURE SAYS ONLY A FEW WORDS: HIGH WIND DOES NOT LAST LONG, NOR DOES HEAVY RAIN.

IF NATURE'S WORDS DO NOT LAST WHY SHOULD THOSE OF MAN?

二十三

You talk too much

—the Book of the Nomad

EXPERIENCE IS A RIVERBED,
ITS SOURCE HIDDEN, FOREVER FLOWING:
ITS ENTRANCE, THE ROOT OF THE WORLD,
THE WAY MOVES WITHIN IT:
DRAW UPON IT; IT WILL NOT RUN DRY.

Little hand says it's time to rock and roll.

—the Book of Bodhi

WHEN RULERS TAKE GRAIN SO THAT THEY MAY FEAST, THEIR PEOPLE BECOME HUNGRY

七十四

Nobody Puts Baby in the Corner

--the Book of Johnny Castle

**CAUTIOUS AS ONE CROSSING THIN ICE,
UNDECIDED AS ONE SURROUNDED BY DANGER,
MODEST AS ONE WHO IS A GUEST.**

十五

People who really wanna have a good time won't come to a slaughter house

—the Book of Dalton

**WITHOUT TAKING A STEP OUTDOORS,
YOU KNOW THE WHOLE WORLD;**

**WITHOUT TAKING A PEEP OUT THE WINDOW
YOU KNOW THE COLOR OF THE SKY.**

四十七

You shouldn't play with sharp objects.

―the Book of the Nomad

MEN FLOW INTO LIFE, AND EBB INTO DEATH.
SOME ARE FILLED WITH LIFE;
SOME ARE EMPTY WITH DEATH;
SOME HOLD FAST TO LIFE, AND THEREBY PERISH,
FOR LIFE IS AN ABSTRACTION.

五十

It is not tragic to die doing what you love

—the Book of Bodhi

SO THE STRONG MUST GUIDE THE WEAK,
FOR THE WEAK ARE RAW MATERIAL TO THE STRONG.
IF THE GUIDE IS NOT RESPECTED,
OR THE MATERIAL IS NOT CARED FOR,
CONFUSION WILL RESULT...

NO MATTER HOW CLEVER ONE IS.

二十七

When you grow up... then you'll know these things, Danny. Now get up here and piss in the radiator.

—the Book of Jed

**WHO RECOGNIZES HIS LIMITATIONS IS HEALTHY;
WHO IGNORES HIS LIMITATIONS IS SICK.
THE SAGE RECOGNIZES THIS SICKNESS AS A LIMITATION.
AND SO BECOMES IMMUNE.**

Pain don't hurt.

—the Book of Dalton

A JOURNEY OF A THOUSAND MILES BEGINS AT THE SPOT UNDER ONE'S FEET

六十四

Everyone is a wanderer these days

—the Book of the Nomad

FOR EVEN THE STRONGEST FORCE WILL WEAKEN WITH TIME, AND THEN ITS VIOLENCE WILL RETURN, AND KILL IT.

三十

I want you to be nice, until it's time to not be nice.

—the Book of Dalton

BOTH PRAISE AND BLAME CAUSE CONCERN,
FOR THEY BRING PEOPLE HOPE AND FEAR.
THE OBJECT OF HOPE AND FEAR IS THE SELF -
FOR, WITHOUT SELF, TO WHOM MAY FORTUNE
AND DISASTER OCCUR?

十三

You can't be a coward and be number one.

—the Book of Ace

**WHO UNDERSTANDS DOES NOT PREACH;
WHO PREACHES DOES NOT UNDERSTAND.**

五十六

When I need advice on how to take care of one kid brother, I'll ask my other kid brother.

—the Book of Darry

**THERE IS NO GREATER MISTAKE THAN FOLLOWING DESIRE;
THERE IS NO GREATER DISASTER THAN FORGETTING CONTENTMENT;
THERE IS NO GREATER SICKNESS THAN SEEKING ATTAINMENT;
BUT ONE WHO IS CONTENT TO SATISFY HIS NEEDS
FINDS THAT CONTENTMENT ENDURES.**

四十一

Those looking for **trouble** are not much of a **problem** to someone ready for them.

—the Book of Dalton

TOO MUCH COLOUR BLINDS THE EYE,
TOO MUCH MUSIC DEAFENS THE EAR,
TOO MUCH TASTE DULLS THE PALATE,
TOO MUCH PLAY MADDENS THE MIND,
TOO MUCH DESIRE TEARS THE HEART.

十二

Good-looking people turn me off. Myself included.

---the Book of Patrick

WHEN THE GREAT MAN LEARNS THE WAY, HE FOLLOWS IT WITH DILIGENCE;
WHEN THE COMMON MAN LEARNS THE WAY, HE FOLLOWS IT ON OCCASION;
WHEN THE MEAN MAN LEARNS THE WAY, HE LAUGHS OUT LOUD;
THOSE WHO DO NOT LAUGH, DO NOT LEARN AT ALL

四十一

The Steps aren't enough

—the Book of Johnny Castle

WHAT IS THE DIFFERENCE BETWEEN ASSENT AND DENIAL?
WHAT IS THE DIFFERENCE BETWEEN BEAUTIFUL AND UGLY?
WHAT IS THE DIFFERENCE BETWEEN FEARSOME AND AFRAID?

Too many young men and women are paralyzed by their fears.

—the Book of Darko

**SO SLAUGHTERS MUST BE MOURNED
AND CONQUEST CELEBRATED WITH A FUNERAL.**

三十一

No one ever wins a fight.

—the Book of Dalton

**THE SAGE ACCEPTS THE WORLD
AS THE WORLD ACCEPTS THE WAY.**

二十二

Ditto.

—the Book of Sam Wheat

**EMPTY THE SELF COMPLETELY;
LET THE MIND BECOME STILL.
THE WORLD WILL RISE AND MOVE;
WHILE THE SELF WATCHES THEIR RETURN.**

Don't look down.

—the Book of Johnny Castle

BIBLIOGRAPHY

This book attempts to draw the texts of several popular English translations of Lao Tse into a consistent and accessible context. It is based on a blend of the translations of Robert G. Henricks, Lin Yutang, D.C. Lau, Ch'u Ta-Kao, Gia-Fu Feng & Jane English, Richard Wilhelm and Aleister Crowley.

THE SWAYZE QUOTES

THE BOOK OF ACE
Skate Town USA-Nick Castle
(KBC & Rastar Pictures)

THE BOOK OF BODHI
Point Break-Rick King & W. Peter Iliff
(Largo Entertainment & Twentieth Century-Fox Film Corporation)

THE BOOK OF DALTON
Road House-David Lee Henry
(Silver Pictures & Star Partners II Ltd., United Artists & MGM/UA Home Entertainment)

THE BOOK OF DARKO
Donnie Darko-Richard Kelly
(Flower Films, Adam Fields Productions, Gaylord Films and Newmarket Films, in association with Pandora Cinema, 20th Century Fox Home Entertainment)

THE BOOK OF DARRY
the Outsiders-S.E. Hinton & Kathleen Rowell
(Pony Boy Productions & Zoetrope Studios Warner Bros. Pictures & Warner Home Video)

THE SWAYZE QUOTES

THE BOOK OF JED
Red Dawn-John Milius
(United Artists & Valkyrie Films
MGM/UA Entertainment Company & MGM/UA Home Entertainment)

THE BOOK OF JOHNNY CASTLE
Dirty Dancing-Eleanor Bergstein
(Great American Films Limited Partnership & Vestron Pictures
Artisan Entertainment)

THE BOOK OF THE NOMAD
Steel Dawn-Doug Lefler
(Yellowpine Ltd. Artisan Entertainment, Silver Lion Films, Vestron Pictures & Vestron Video)

THE BOOK OF PATRICK
Patrick Swayze

THE BOOK OF VIDA
To Wong Foo, Thanks for Everything Julie Newmar-Douglas Carter Beane
(Universal Pictures)

THE BOOK OF SAM WHEAt
Ghost-Bruce Joel Rubin
(Paramount Pictures)

PROCEEDS

Vicious Books will donate proceeds from reported sales of the book, *Nobody Puts Swayze in the Corner: the Tao of Swayze,* to the American Cancer Society on a Quarterly basis.

Vicious Books is not affiliated with the American Cancer Society. All donations will be made through the American Cancer Society's website as a general donation from the publisher.

SPECIAL NOTE

This book is a rather fictional concept written by a completely fictional person who hails from another work of fiction, the novel *Rorschach's Ribs* by Marcus Eder. If you are intrigued by the ambiguous existence of a thoroughly non-living author and would like to know what sort of events would lead to his creation of a somewhat real book (though originally published in a fictional world born out of the troubled, somewhat dusty mind of an assumed, real-life mad man) do run out and purchase the novel, *Rorschach's Ribs*, by Marcus Eder at your earliest discourse and leisure. *Rorschach's Ribs* can be found online at fine purveyors of fiction throughout the country, or additionally through the publisher, Vicious Books.

ABOUT VICIOUS BOOKS

Vicious Books is an alternative, independent press located in St. Louis, Missouri, specializing in literary fiction, poetry, philosophy and pretty much anything else that floats our boat.

Vicious Books publishes 2-3 titles per year, focused on bringing an honest voice to the mainstream while remaining on the fringe; remaining independent.

Every now again we even try to do something good for this crazy mixed-up world of ours.

Vicious Books publishes the type of literature the mainstream is afraid of. The type of literature that hasn't been published a million times before.

For more information visit www.viciousbooks.com

BE SURE TO CHECK OUT THE OTHER AUTHORS AND TITLES FROM VICIOUS BOOKS AS WELL AS USEFUL LINKS, NEWS AND MORE AT

WWW.VICIOUSBOOKS.COM

CPSIA information can be obtained at www.ICGtesting.com
Printed in the USA
BVOW012138010512

289194BV00005B/2/P